# *Flash Revise*
## *Pocketbook*

## AS/A-Level Geography
Human Geography

Philip Allan Updates, an imprint of Hodder Education, an Hachette UK company, Market Place, Deddington, Oxfordshire OX15 0SE

**Orders**

Bookpoint Ltd, 130 Milton Park, Abingdon, Oxfordshire OX14 4SB
tel: 01235 827720     fax: 01235 400454     e-mail: uk.orders@bookpoint.co.uk

Lines are open 9.00 a.m.–5.00 p.m., Monday to Saturday, with a 24-hour message answering service. You can also order through our website: www.philipallan.co.uk

© Philip Allan Updates 2010
ISBN 978-1-4441-0780-7

First published in 2004 as *Flashrevise Cards*

Impression number  5  4  3  2  1
Year    2015    2014    2013    2012    2011    2010

All rights reserved; no part of this publication may be reproduced, stored in a retrieval system, or transmitted, in any other form or by any means, electronic, mechanical, photocopying, recording or otherwise without either the prior written permission of Philip Allan Updates or a licence permitting restricted copying in the United Kingdom issued by the Copyright Licensing Agency Ltd, Saffron House, 6–10 Kirby Street, London EC1N 8TS.

Printed in Spain

Hachette UK's policy is to use papers that are natural, renewable and recyclable products and made from wood grown in sustainable forests. The logging and manufacturing processes are expected to conform to the environmental regulations of the country of origin.

P01650

# Population distribution

**Q1** Which continent has over half the world's population?

**Q2** Which continent is home to the fewest people?

**Q3** Which two terms are used to describe the uneven spread of population and economic activity between two regions of a nation?

**Q4** Why might governments try to spread population more evenly?

**ANSWERS**

A1 Asia

A2 Antarctica

A3 Core and periphery

A4 Congestion in the core; undeveloped resources in the periphery;
strategic/military reasons

*examiner's* **note** Indicate the significance of data when comparing numbers
of people living in different regions. Think of the 'headline' that a newspaper
might use to report these data. It would employ comparative language to convey
some sense of magnitude and significance rather than simply stating the figures.
For instance, 1.3 billion people live in China: this is *one-fifth* of the world's total
population (6.8 billion); it is *more than 20 times greater* than the UK's population
(61 million).

( 1 ) **ANSWERS**

# Population density

**Q1** Name the two most densely populated continents.

**Q2** Which factor has the greatest direct influence on global variations in population density?

**Q3** Suggest two human influences on population density in rural areas.

**Q4** Suggest two influences on population density in urban areas.

ANSWERS

# the number of people per unit area of land

**A1** Asia and Europe

**A2** Climate (and associated global vegetation and soil types). Over half the world's population still lives directly off the land and harsh physical environments almost always have low population densities.

**A3** Choose from: proximity to markets and transport routes; use of irrigation or other agricultural technology; tourist appeal of the area

**A4** Choose from: land values; council housing and slum clearance schemes; parks; rivers and their floodplains

*examiner's* **note** Climate is the key control when explaining global patterns but human influences are much clearer at the local scale. Market forces, transport routes and political actions all produce microscale variations in density within broadly defined climatic regions.

(2) **ANSWERS**

# Crude death rate (CDR)

**Q1** Estimate the CDR for (a) western Europe, (b) sub-Saharan Africa.

**Q2** Estimate the life expectancy for men and women in (a) western Europe, (b) sub-Saharan Africa.

**Q3** CDR falls over time due to the improvements in h............, h............ and f............ s............ brought about by economic development.

**Q4** Provide supporting details for your answers to question 3.

**ANSWERS**

## the number of deaths per 1000 people per year

A1 (a) 9–11 per 1000 per year     (b) 15–25 per 1000 per year

A2 (a) Men: 70–77; women: 78–84     (b) Men: 40–50; women: 45–55

A3 Hygiene, health, food supply

A4 Sewers, clean water and personal cleanliness contribute to improved hygiene; healthcare includes both preventive medicine and surgery; intensification and extensification of farming improve food supply, as do imports

***examiner's* note** Higher birth rates in the UK in the past have resulted in a large proportion of people now being aged over 65. As these people reach the end of their life span, a higher proportion of the population dies each year. The UK's CDR is increasing as a result. Do not attribute this rise in deaths to an epidemic or disaster. Life expectancy and levels of health are higher than ever.

# Crude birth rate (CBR)

**Q1** Estimate the CBR for (a) western Europe, (b) sub-Saharan Africa.

**Q2** State two social factors that help determine the CBR.

**Q3** Why do births decline as levels of primary-sector employment (farming) fall?

**Q4** How does the total fertility rate (TFR) differ from the CBR? Why is it sometimes regarded as a more useful measure?

**ANSWERS** ▶▶

## the number of live births per 1000 people per year

**A1** (a) 10–15 per 1000 per year    (b) 45–50 per 1000 per year

**A2** Choose from: contraceptive use and sex education; women's rights; school-leaving age; strength of religious beliefs

**A3** Subsistence farming uses children as a source of labour, whereas in a developed society too many children can become a financial burden

**A4** TFR is the total number of children a woman has in her lifetime. Unlike the CBR, it is independent of population structure and therefore a better measure of social 'development'.

***examiner's* note** Influences on birth rate are just as applicable to variations between regions of a country or different ethnic groups as they are to national differences. Use of supporting data and place names always gains more credit than simple reference to 'high' or 'low' births and 'rich' or 'poor' places.

 **ANSWERS**

# Natural increase

**Q1** The birth rate in Sierra Leone is 48 per 1000 per year while the death rate is only 23 per 1000 per year. What is the rate of natural increase?

**Q2** What other process can cause a population to change size?

**Q3** Why might rates of natural increase fluctuate from year to year within a country?

**Q4** Why are rates of natural increase still so high in many low-income nations?

ANSWERS

## the annual growth rate of a population calculated by subtracting the death rate from the birth rate

**A1** 25 per 1000 per year (or 2.5%)

**A2** Migration

**A3** An economic recession, political crisis, war, epidemic disease or famine might affect the levels of births and/or deaths

**A4** Science has improved health and food supply while pre-industrial (highly religious) attitudes towards use of contraception and family size still prevail. Hence births are significantly higher than deaths.

***examiner's* note** Changes in rates of natural increase over time are often presented in graphical form for descriptive analysis. A thorough description will:
• state the overall picture — perhaps rates have doubled or halved over time
• identify any significant period of acceleration or deceleration of growth
• highlight any short-term anomalies

 **ANSWERS**

# Demographic transition model (DTM)

**Q1** Name the four stages of the DTM.

**Q2** How does natural increase change through the four stages of the DTM?

**Q3** When, approximately, did the UK enter the period of population growth shown in the model?

**Q4** Upon what evidence is the DTM based?

ANSWERS

## the pattern of change in population that occurs in response to industrialisation

**A1** High stationary, early expanding, late expanding and low stationary

**A2** No growth occurs until the beginning of stage 2. It rises to a maximum at the end of stage 2 and thereafter population increases but at a decreasing rate. Growth ends with the onset of stage 4.

**A3** Between 1750 and 1780

**A4** Population data for northern Europe, sourced from parish (church) registers and national census records

*examiner's* **note** Some accounts of the model suggest a fifth stage in which population falls because of a very low birth rate.

**ANSWERS**

# Population structure

**Q1** How is the age–sex structure of a population best displayed?

**Q2** What is an ethnic minority group?

**Q3** Which term has largely replaced the word 'class' when discussing income and status differences in the UK?

**Q4** Suggest three contrasting ways in which population structure varies between urban and rural areas in the UK.

ANSWERS

## the make-up of a population according to criteria such as age–sex, income or ethnicity

A1 By constructing an age–sex pyramid

A2 A sub-group of the population which has religious beliefs, a spoken language or skin colour not shared by the wider majority

A3 Socioeconomic group (SEG)

A4 • Greater ethnic diversity in large cities
   • Rural populations tend to be older
   • Greater range of incomes in urban areas

***examiner's* note** Questions that ask about changes in population structure or 'population characteristics' are very common and are often linked with the processes of urbanisation or migration. Try to offer a wide interpretation of structure and not just a narrow account of changes to the age–sex composition of the population. Notably, population employment structures are radically modified by urbanisation.

 **7** **ANSWERS**

# Age–sex pyramid

**Q1** What is the name for the age–sex groups used in a pyramid?

**Q2** What demographic characteristic is indicated by concave sides on a national age–sex pyramid?

**Q3** What 'irregularity' would appear in an age–sex pyramid for a city in an LEDC? Why?

**Q4** How are pyramids for some UK coastal resorts modified by retirement migration?

ANSWERS

A1 Cohorts

A2 A high death rate (as many people are not surviving between generations)

A3 Rural–urban migration increases the size of the 15–40 cohort, especially males

A4 Up to 40% are over 60 (the figure for the UK as a whole is 21%)

***examiner's* note** Do not confuse the impact of migration with rates of natural increase. A New Town such as Milton Keynes has a similarly shaped pyramid to a typical LEDC. However, this is because of the selective in-migration of young families with children and the fact that few elderly people have chosen to live there. It certainly does not mean that there is high mortality in Milton Keynes. In contrast, national pyramids should be treated primarily as a product of birth and death rates.

# Youthful population

**Q1** Estimate the percentage of the population that is under 15 in (a) western Europe, (b) sub-Saharan Africa

**Q2** Why do pre-industrial societies with high crude birth rates seldom have a very youthful population?

**Q3** What are the *short-term* economic costs of a youthful population?

**Q4** Suggest a *long-term* economic problem.

ANSWERS

## a population in which the average age has fallen and a high proportion is aged under 15

**A1** (a) Between 15% and 20%    (b) Between 45% and 50%

**A2** High infant mortality means few children survive infancy

**A3** Young people are dependent on others for necessities such as food and clothing. Schooling and healthcare costs force tax rises.

**A4** In 50 years' time there will be a large elderly population requiring medical care, housing and basic pensions; this is occurring in the UK, with the postwar 'baby boomers' now reaching the age of 65

***examiner's* note** Look for evidence of an 'echo' of a previous youthful population. For instance, the end of the Second World War resulted in a baby boom in America in the 1950s. Subsequently, there was an 'echo' of increased births in the 1980s as the baby boomers grew up to have their own children. Similarly, low births during the world wars resulted in an echo of decreased births 30 years later.

 **ANSWERS**

# Ageing population

**Q1** How can an ageing population be identified on an age–sex pyramid?

**Q2** Why are European populations ageing?

**Q3** Why might some local areas have a larger elderly population than others?

**Q4** What economic and social costs are associated with an ageing population?

ANSWERS

# a population in which the average age is increasing

**A1** Relatively high numbers are aged 60 and over (now 21% in the UK and up to twice this in popular retirement towns)

**A2** Improving health is accompanied by a continued decline in births. Consequently, a greater proportion of the population is now older.

**A3** Selective migration of retired people to coastal and scenic areas increases the proportion found there while leaving fewer elsewhere

**A4** Increased taxation to support subsidised health services; entertainment facilities for the young may be lacking

***examiner's* note** Structure an extended answer to consider positive as well as negative effects. The elderly provide jobs in service and care industries (an example of a multiplier effect). They bring experience to a job (the fields of politics, drama and literature bring to mind people who work into their eighties and even nineties).

**(10)** ANSWERS

# Dependency ratio

**Q1** Dependency ratio $= \dfrac{\text{no. of children (1–14) and elderly (over 65)}}{\text{no. of working age (15–65)}}$

Calculate the UK's dependency ratio if 65% are aged 15–65.

**Q2** Why is 15 an unrealistic lower limit of dependency in MEDCs?

**Q3** Why do people work beyond the age of 65 in many LEDCs?

**Q4** LEDC statistics might overestimate dependency because many young and elderly people work in the i................ sector.

**ANSWERS** ▶▶

# the ratio of non–productive people to economically active adults in a population

A1  35/65 = 0.54 (sometimes this ratio is multiplied by 100)

A2  Many people stay on at school and university to the age of 21 or older and so do not generate earnings until much later in life

A3  Many LEDCs lack a state-funded pension scheme and people must keep working until they are physically unable to continue

A4  Informal

*examiner's* **note** Dependency ratios are hard to measure in LEDCs where many children work from an early age while the elderly never really retire because of lack of pensions. In contrast, universal entitlement to a state pension at the age of 65 (or 60 for women) was introduced in the UK as part of the Welfare State in 1945. A clearer dependency line can thus be drawn.

# Census

**Q1** How often is the national census conducted in the UK and when did it begin?

**Q2** Why is the census more accurate than any other social survey?

**Q3** What is the smallest geographical scale for which census data are made available in the UK?

**Q4** What historical data can be used that pre-date the national census?

ANSWERS

**A1** Every 10 years since 1801, excluding 1941

**A2** Other surveys provide estimates based upon samples. By law, everyone must participate in the national census.

**A3** Ward (about 5000 households) or enumeration district (about 500)

**A4** Parish church registers of burials, baptisms and marriages

*examiner's* **note** Towards the end of each 10-year period, the data can become inaccurate as they no longer reflect reality. This is especially true for urban areas that experience the rapid social and economic changes associated with gentrification (when in-migrating affluent groups displace poorer sections of the local community).

# Population policy

**Q1** Which Asian country introduced a one-child policy in 1980?

**Q2** How has this policy recently been modified?

**Q3** Why might a government encourage more births?

**Q4** How are population policies enforced?

## an act of government that aims to reduce or increase population growth rates

A1 China

A2 Two children are now permitted in rural areas, or if the first child born to a family is a girl or disabled

A3 To counter underpopulation; to increase its labour supply; to tackle ageing population

A4 Financial penalties and rewards, usually linked to the award of state benefits. In Nazi Germany medals were awarded to the mothers of three or more children.

*examiner's* **note** If asked how political factors influence population growth, an alternative approach could be to examine the indirect impact of education, health and welfare policies. The raising of school leaving age, the provision of pensions and the legalisation of contraception and abortion have all contributed to near-zero growth in the UK.

# Natural resources

**Q1** What name is given to resources such as oil and coal that are only replaceable on a time-scale of millions of years?

**Q2** Greater use of renewable resources (such as solar and tidal power) is vital if s............ development is to be achieved.

**Q3** Suggest two ways in which a society might increase its level of natural resources.

**Q4** What other types of resource are there?

ANSWERS

## parts of the physical environment that are used to satisfy human needs and wants

A1 Non-renewable

A2 Sustainable

A3 Discovery of new reserves of an existing resource, such as oil; technological breakthrough that allows new power sources to be identified; imports; annexing new resource-rich territory

A4 Human resources (labour and its skills) and material resources (machinery and the built environment)

***examiner's* note** Resources are a 'relational' concept. This means they are only defined as such when they are discovered to be useful. For instance, it was only with the invention of the petrol engine that oil was perceived to have real value. This can be summed up in the saying 'resources are not; they become'.

# Overpopulation

**Q1** State an economic consequence of overpopulation.

**Q2** State a social consequence of overpopulation.

**Q3** State a political consequence of overpopulation.

**Q4** What can solve the problem of overpopulation other than a reduction in the number of people?

ANSWERS

## too many people relative to the resources available to maintain high standards of living

**A1** High unemployment; negative balance of trade (over-dependence on imports); low wages (due to a large 'reserve army of labour')

**A2** Malnourishment and spread of disease; civil war may be fought over resources; high levels of emigration

**A3** Population control policies; anti-immigration rules; unstable regime

**A4** The discovery of new resources; greater levels of imports; increase in food yields through agricultural intensification and extensification

***examiner's* note** Examiners look for clear understanding that there is no such thing as 'too many people'. Overpopulation is a 'relational' concept. This means that population numbers are being examined in relation to the size of a resource base that is not permanently fixed in size and that can always be increased through scientific endeavour, trade or aid.

 **ANSWERS**

# Underpopulation

**Q1** State a political consequence of underpopulation.

**Q2** State an economic consequence of underpopulation.

**Q3** Why might an area become underpopulated other than through a fall in the number of people living there?

**Q4** What is meant by optimum population?

ANSWERS

# too few people in an area to use the resources efficiently at current levels of technology

A1 Pro-immigration or pro-natalist policies

A2 Low profits as firms struggle to achieve an economy of scale; high wages due to labour shortages; high taxes to subsidise public services

A3 New resources are found or demand grows for new services (such as tourism). Neither opportunity is exploited due to labour shortages.

A4 Optimum population is the theoretical population that, when working with all the available resources, will maximise standards of living

***examiner's* note** Areas with a low population density, such as deserts, are not necessarily underpopulated. If an area possesses very few resources, then an increase in population numbers would not be beneficial to anyone. Underpopulation only exists where low population density is resulting in an actual neglect of valuable resources that have the potential, if exploited, to raise standards of living for everyone.

 **ANSWERS**

# Malthus's theory

**Q1** What is meant by geometric growth of population and arithmetic growth of food resources?

**Q2** Once population growth outstrips food supply, then 'positive checks' may occur. These are f............, d............ and w............

**Q3** What is meant by the term 'ceiling to growth'?

**Q4** Malthus's theory dates from 1798. What was the main 'preventive check' to population growth at this time?

ANSWERS

**A1** Population doubles each generation (2, 4, 8, 16...) whereas food supply increases by a constant amount (e.g. 1, 2, 3, 4, 5...)

**A2** Famine, disease and war

**A3** The upper limit to population numbers determined by the level of food production

**A4** A later age of marriage, thereby limiting potential family sizes

***examiner's* note** Malthus could not have foreseen the growth of secular (non-religious) thinking that has resulted in legalised abortion and freely available contraception. Equally, food supply has actually kept apace with world population growth because of advancements in agricultural science, such as the Green Revolution. Consequently, positive checks have thus far been avoided by many (but not all) nations.

**(17) ANSWERS**

# Boserup's theory

**Q1** Compared with the pessimism of Malthus, Boserup's theory is considered to be an o............... approach to population growth.

**Q2** Boserup's theory is summarised by which old saying?

**Q3** Boserup argues that population pressure results in a reduction in the length of time for which fields are left fallow (uncultivated). This is an example of the i............... of farming methods.

**Q4** Why is population growth a 'positive' force in her model?

ANSWERS

## population growth stimulates changes in agriculture that allow more food to be produced

A1 Optimistic

A2 'Necessity is the mother of invention'

A3 Intensification

A4 Population pressure is encouraging innovation that might otherwise not occur

***examiner's* note** Boserup's theory is based upon convincing field evidence suggesting that population growth encourages crop rotation and changes in land tenure. Such reforms occur only when the threat of population pressure is evident and the carrying capacity of the land is about to be exceeded. Over time, she envisages a series of sudden leaps forward in the scale of food production. By contrast, Malthus foresaw farming improvements as occurring at a constant rate, albeit slowly.

# Migration

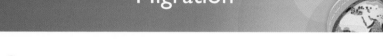

**Q1** T............. and c............. are temporary movements that should not be classed as migration.

**Q2** What is meant by net migration?

**Q3** In terms of sheer volume, what is by far the largest single type of migration flow? Provide some supporting evidence.

**Q4** A migrant's decision-making process involves careful weighing of the c............. and b............. of moving.

ANSWERS

## movement of people that results in a permanent or semi-permanent change of address

A1 Tourism and commuting

A2 The annual balance between levels of immigration and emigration that results in an overall loss or gain in numbers

A3 Movement of economic migrants from rural to urban areas in LEDCs (rural–urban migration). Since 1950, the world's urban population has grown from 0.8 billion to 2.9 billion. Migration fuels this growth (although high fertility is also important).

A4 Costs and benefits

*examiner's* **note** When writing about the 'consequences' of migration, cover economic, social, cultural, demographic and environmental themes. Impacts can be felt at the origin, the destination and across a whole region (through the intensification of regional disparities, the spread of disease or the diffusion of new attitudes).

# Economic migration

**Q1** What are the negative consequences of rural–urban migration for low-income nations?

**Q2** Are international labour migrants rich or poor?

**Q3** Seasonal movement for work is a form of t............. migration.

**Q4** Economic migrants may send their wages back to family members in their country of origin. The money is called a r.............

ANSWERS

## voluntary movement of people in search of improved conditions of work and pay

A1 Overcrowding and shanty-town growth in cities; possible abandonment of an elderly dependent population in rural areas

A2 Both. Poor unskilled workers do seek entry to MEDCs (to the USA from Mexico, for instance). However, international migrants can also be highly skilled software developers, doctors and academics (a 'brain drain'), as well as top-level footballers or actors.

A3 Temporary

A4 Remittance

***examiner's* note** An account of the consequences of labour migration should be structured carefully. There are positive and negative consequences for the individuals involved, the societies they have left and the societies they are entering. These consequences can be economic, social, demographic or environmental.

# Refugees

**Q1** What are possible physical causes of refugee movements?

**Q2** What are possible political causes of refugee movements?

**Q3** Political refugees in search of safety are also called a..............
s...............

**Q4** Why are some countries more likely than others to welcome refugees?

ANSWERS

**A1** Tectonic hazards (volcanoes and earthquakes); hydro-meteorological hazards (storms, floods and drought); sea-level rise

**A2** Genocide; ethnic cleansing or large-scale conflict

**A3** Asylum seekers

**A4** Certain countries welcome refugees who share their religion or language; some governments are more sympathetic than others

***examiner's* note** Countries with strong economies may be attractive to refugees but they will not necessarily be allowed entry. Remember that the decisions taken by a country's government determine how many refugees are allowed entry, not the strength of economic pull factors.

**(21)** **ANSWERS**

# Rural–urban migration

**Q1** What is the primary cause of large-scale rural–urban migration?

**Q2** What additional push factors operate?

**Q3** What pull factors attract migrants to urban areas?

**Q4** When did widespread urbanisation begin in western Europe?

**ANSWERS**

**A1** Overpopulation in rural areas (resulting from high rates of natural increase as modern medicine and improvements in food supply reduce mortality rates)

**A2** Modernisation of agriculture leaves many peasants landless; natural hazards or civil war could contribute

**A3** The prospect of employment; healthcare and education are also likely to be better

**A4** Between 1750 and 1800

***examiner's* note** Viewed globally, this is the most significant form of migration. However, in the majority of MEDCs, population growth through natural increase has ceased and so too has rural–urban migration. Increasingly, the flow has reversed and rural areas have experienced repopulation. This is known as counter-urbanisation.

# Lee's model

**Q1** Distinguish between push and pull factors.

**Q2** What are intervening obstacles?

**Q3** Suggest some commonly perceived intervening obstacles for potential migrants.

**Q4** What is an intervening opportunity?

ANSWERS ▶▶

# a representation of migration in terms of push and pull factors and intervening obstacles

**A1** Push factors repel migrants from their previous location, while pull factors draw them to their new homes

**A2** Barriers to movement. While these can be physical, such as a river, Lee focused upon social and economic obstacles to migration.

**A3** Removal costs; abandonment of friends and family; fear and uncertainty

**A4** Associated with Stouffer (1940), this can refer to places on the route that might divert the migrant from his/her original destination

***examiner's* note** Lee's (1966) model is an improvement over simple push–pull ideas, as it emphasises the importance of individual decision-making. People of differing ages, incomes and personality characteristics will perceive the challenges and opportunities of migration differently. The model can explain 'irrational' behaviour, where people do not migrate despite there being benefits in doing so.

# Primary sector

**Q1** Name the five types of primary work.

**Q2** Why do primary-based economies often have low rates of growth?

**Q3** Why are primary-based economies sometimes described as 'vulnerable'?

**Q4** Why are primary-producing nations often unhappy with global terms of trade?

ANSWERS

# production of food, fuel and raw materials

**A1** Mining, farming, forestry, fishing and energy (e.g. wind and hydroelectric power)

**A2** Processing is needed to add value to many primary products

**A3** Materials run out or are replaced by new inventions (plastics have largely replaced tin foil); natural hazards can destroy crops and forests; overproduction can depress prices (e.g. coffee)

**A4** The World Trade Organization encourages free trade of manufactured goods but allows protectionism in primary markets

***examiner's* note** The Organization of Petroleum Exporting Countries (OPEC), formed in 1973, is a rare example of a producer cartel made up of previously poor countries successfully working together to improve greatly their terms of trade. They collectively raised oil prices by over 400% in 1973. Nations such as Saudi Arabia are extremely rich because of oil.

# Secondary sector

**Q1** What name is given to manufacturing industries that simply refine raw materials (such as the steel industry)?

**Q2** What name is given to manufacturing industries that produce items such as 'white goods', cars or televisions?

**Q3** What is an assembly industry?

**Q4** Assembly of microprocessors to make computers is a form of manufacturing. In which sector do their designers work?

ANSWERS

A1 Processing industries (many are also examples of heavy industry)

A2 Consumer industries (or consumer goods industries)

A3 Any manufacturing industry that takes the products of another industry and fits them together to make finished goods

A4 Quaternary sector

***examiner's* note** The secondary sector is clearly very diverse — try to emphasise this. Great variety exists in both the locational demands of industries (some are tied to raw materials, others to a labour force or a market) and the skill levels and wages of the workers. For instance, skilled craftsmen who build furniture by hand are often highly paid.

**(25) ANSWERS**

# Tertiary sector

**Q1** Banks and solicitors are examples of what kind of services?

**Q2** Retailers and hotels are examples of what kind of services?

**Q3** What is the dominant geographical trend among tertiary industries in high-income nations? Why?

**Q4** What is a national shift from secondary to tertiary employment called?

ANSWERS

A1 Producer services

A2 Consumer services

A3 Decentralisation (relocating from inner urban areas to fringe areas such as retail parks); this reflects rising costs in city centres and has been aided by growth in transport networks

A4 Tertiarisation (or post-industrialisation)

***examiner's* note** A vast range of pay and skill differences exists — producer services often employ very high-salaried workers, consumer services less so. Public (government) sector pay is highly varied too. Tertiarisation does not automatically follow a decline in manufacturing. Mass unemployment can depress consumer spending, as happened in the Great Depression of the 1930s.

# Quaternary sector

**Q1** Apart from information technology, what are the other main areas of quaternary work?

**Q2** What is the most important quaternary resource?

**Q3** How does the physical environment influence the location of quaternary activities?

**Q4** The design of microprocessors is quaternary work. The mass-production of computers belongs to which sector of work?

ANSWERS

**A1** Pharmaceuticals, biotechnology, aerospace industries, new media

**A2** A highly skilled (often postgraduate level) workforce found near leading universities and government research facilities

**A3** Skilled workers can make demands for a pleasant working environment, often in an unspoilt out-of-town location

**A4** Secondary

***examiner's* note** The dividing line between tertiary and quaternary work is thin. Providing information derived from new research could also be reasonably classed as a service. Equally, senior office managers who devise new corporate strategies could perhaps be said to be quaternary workers. For these reasons, quaternary work is often referred to as a 'sub-set' of the tertiary sector.

# Sector growth model

**Q1** Name the four sectors of industry shown in the model.

**Q2** Describe the employment structure of a pre-industrial society.

**Q3** Which sector dominates during the industrial period? Why?

**Q4** Describe the employment structure of a post-industrial society.

ANSWERS ▶▶

# the shift in the proportions employed in different sectors as a region develops

A1 Primary, secondary, tertiary and quaternary

A2 The majority (over two-thirds) work in primary industry with a small proportion in secondary and tertiary work

A3 Secondary; initially, these manufacturing industries are likely to be labour-intensive (later they may become mechanised and capital-intensive)

A4 The majority are tertiary workers, with secondary work falling. Fewer than 5% are primary workers and quaternary may exceed this.

***examiner's* note** The Fisher–Clark model (as it is also known) shows employment figures, not output or profits. Although less than 2% of the UK workforce is now in agriculture, output is higher than in pre-industrial times, because of mechanisation. Although the number employed in manufacturing might fall, profits for firms may be increasing as branch plants are relocated overseas where labour costs are lower.

# Globalisation

**Q1** What general term describes industries that operate on a global scale?

**Q2** What technological changes have particularly helped bring about deeper globalisation?

**Q3** Suggest some social consequences of globalisation.

**Q4** Suggest some economic consequences of globalisation.

**ANSWERS**

## the widening and deepening of economic, political and cultural linkages between nations

A1 Transnational corporations (TNCs)

A2 Reduced flight times and costs of air travel; containerised shipping; improved communication technologies (internet)

A3 Increases in international labour migrations; spread of 'Western values' and US culture; growth of anti-global protests and reactive terrorism; growth of new online 'cyber-communities'

A4 'Global shift' of manufacturing jobs from MEDCs to LEDCs; economic polarisation of richest and poorest nations; increased global GDP

***examiner's* note** Globalisation can be seen in both a positive and negative light. Critics point to the low wages that workers in LEDCs are paid to assemble goods for sale in MEDCs. Yet previously, many would have toiled as subsistence farmers. Which is the lesser of the two ills?

(29) ANSWERS

# Global networks

**Q1** What is a node?

**Q2** What are the most important nodes called? Give an example.

**Q3** Why are some places relatively 'switched off' from global networks?

**Q4** What is time–space compression?

**ANSWERS** ⟫

**A1** A connected place within a network

**A2** Global hubs; major world cities such as New York, London or Tokyo are global hubs

**A3** They may not be in a strategic location; they may lack a skilled labour force or purchasing power; their governments are politically isolated

**A4** The sense that distant places feel closer than they used to because of improvements in transport and technology

***examiner's* note** Nowhere is entirely switched off from global networks. Poor nations often receive international aid, for instance. It is better to describe poor sub-Saharan nations as experiencing a *shallow* form of integration into global networks that makes them *relatively* switched-off places.

(30) **ANSWERS**

# Global flows

**Q1** What are the main global commodity flows?

**Q2** Why have information and money flows grown rapidly worldwide since the 1980s?

**Q3** Which major transport improvements have helped commodity flows to increase in recent decades?

**Q4** Which important political factors can speed up or slow down different types of flow?

ANSWERS ▶▶

## international movements of people, money, commodities or information that link places together

**A1** Raw materials (including food and energy) and manufactured goods

**A2** Innovation in ICT (information and communications technology) has allowed much faster data and money transfers

**A3** Cheap flights for air-freighted goods and containerised shipping

**A4** Import taxes and duties may reduce commodity trade; immigration rules; internet censorship; regulation of money markets

***examiner's* note** Always try to show good knowledge of current affairs when discussing this topic. The regulation of global flows is a topic of great debate owing to the global 'credit crunch' of 2008. Unregulated money flows led to a boom-and-bust cycle in which major banks lost billions of dollars after a period of risky lending. Global flows of money and commodities slowed down in 2009 for the first time since the Second World War.

# Glocalisation

**Q1** What is 'local sourcing'?

**Q2** Which costs are avoided by using local components?

**Q3** Why do cars have to be assembled differently for sale in US and UK markets?

**Q4** Why do some fast-food items need to be altered for sale in different countries?

ANSWERS

# the local sourcing of parts and customising of products for local markets by TNCs

**A1** Using components from local suppliers to assemble 'global products' closer to the markets where they will be sold (e.g. the US firm Ford's European division builds cars using parts that are made in Europe)

**A2** Import tariffs; greater transport costs

**A3** British cars are right-hand drive and US cars are left-hand drive

**A4** Religious beliefs may affect what meat is eaten; tastes and traditions vary; perishable salads may not always be available

***examiner's* note** Glocalisation is an important aspect of any firm's decision to enter the global marketplace. It helps a firm to be accepted as part of the local business community. Customising the product to meet indigenous tastes might also aid its diffusion into local markets. It is therefore an economic, political and cultural strategy.

(32) **ANSWERS**

# Newly industrialised country (NIC)

**Q1** Name the four 'Asian tigers' of the 1980s.

**Q2** Why does export-orientated manufacturing aid economic and social development?

**Q3** What external factors have aided the growth of NICs?

**Q4** What internal factors have aided the growth of NICs?

ANSWERS

# a former LEDC showing rapid growth in export-orientated manufacturing

**A1** Hong Kong, South Korea, Taiwan, Singapore

**A2** A lot of extra value is added to the product during the manufacturing process, boosting profits. Higher business taxes can then be reinvested in education, health, welfare and infrastructure.

**A3** The arrival of foreign firms seeking cheap labour and new markets; US aid was given to many Asian nations during the Cold War

**A4** Government planning; tariff-free export zones; workforce education; efficient, family-owned firms (called *chaebols* in South Korea)

***examiner's* note** Great variety exists among NICs. Recent additions such as Malaysia are not yet nearly as wealthy as Hong Kong. Growth has slowed in Brazil and Mexico. India has low manufactured exports, relying instead on a huge home market, and has a growing service sector. China is a hybrid capitalist-communist state, now growing at a phenomenal rate.

Some writers call China and India RICs: recently industrialised countries.

# New superpowers

**Q1** Why are India and China becoming important new superpowers?

**Q2** Which two superpowers dominated world affairs from the 1950s until the 1980s?

**Q3** What are the BRICs?

**Q4** What is the G20?

ANSWERS

# nations that have recently begun to have a powerful global influence

A1 Large populations (over 1 billion each); both countries now allow much more foreign investment than they used to

A2 USA and USSR (Russia)

A3 Brazil, Russia, India and China

A4 A grouping of powerful nations that includes both established (USA, EU) and emerging (China, India) superpowers

***examiner's* note** Some geographers used to describe the world as being divided into two groups of countries: more economically developed countries (MEDCs) and less economically developed countries (LEDCs). The emergence of new superpowers such as China, India and the Gulf states means that this older worldview now seems simplistic when discussing world power.

# Transnational corporation (TNC)

**Q1** Which factors could attract a TNC to an LEDC?

**Q2** How might the arrival of a TNC benefit an LEDC?

**Q3** What costs would a US TNC avoid by locating a new branch plant within the European Union?

**Q4** All major TNCs originate in MEDCs. True or false?

ANSWERS

# a firm with operations and interests in more than one country

A1 Cheap labour; weak environmental laws; export-processing zones

A2 Waged labourers stimulate growth in other areas of the economy through their new purchasing power; transfer of technologies; improved skill levels as a result of company training

A3 Tariffs and import quotas

A4 False; some originate in newly industrialised countries (NICs), for example the South Korean firm Daewoo or India's Tata.

***examiner's* note** TNCs are primary shapers of the world economy, with the annual turnover of the largest rivalling the GNP of Norway. With such power comes great responsibility and there are strong arguments both for and against the work of TNCs. Be able to make a reasoned critical judgement that gives equal weight to both sides of the argument.

# Foreign direct investment (FDI)

**Q1** Which political factors deter FDI?

**Q2** Which social factors bring FDI to some countries and not others?

**Q3** Which economic factors bring FDI to some countries and not others?

**Q4** What alternative name is sometimes given to FDI?

ANSWERS

# the extension of operations by a transnational corporation into a new country

**A1** Unstable, corrupt or militant political regimes; communist policies; human rights abuses. However, strict regimes that deter trade union action are sometimes favoured because wages are kept low.

**A2** Spoken language and literacy levels might be important (British firms are establishing call centres in India)

**A3** Low-wage economy; availability of government aid; establishment of a free trade zone (in which exports are exempt from custom duties)

**A4** Inward investment

*examiner's* **note** The majority of FDI actually occurs between MEDCs, rather than between MEDCs and LEDCs. This is due to firms wishing to locate in 'rival' trading blocs in order to reduce import tariffs (e.g. Japanese firm Nissan locating plants in Europe).

# Multiplier effect

**Q1** How does a new economic activity directly stimulate the growth of other firms?

**Q2** In what ways might the workforce of an area stimulate new economic growth?

**Q3** What is the role of the public (government) sector?

**Q4** What is a negative multiplier effect?

ANSWERS

# the beneficial and continuous knock-on effects of economic activity in a region

**A1**  Linked services such as part suppliers or advertisers are needed

**A2**  They spend their wages on goods, services and entertainment

**A3**  Government can tax both businesses and workers. Money is then invested in infrastructure, healthcare and education, thereby attracting even more investment as the region's relative advantage grows.

**A4**  If an industry closes, then there will be associated losses in supply industries and, as unemployment grows, closure of local services and even more job losses, further accelerating decline

***examiner's* note**  The role of the purchasing power of workers should not be overlooked. Leisure demands stimulate growth in other areas of the economy. Simply put, a multiplier effect is the growth of a 'network' of production (making) and consumption (buying).

(37) **ANSWERS**

# Division of labour

**Q1** On an international scale, what division of labour exists?

**Q2** Industries that are free to locate branches wherever labour is cheapest are called f.............. industries.

**Q3** Why has it become easier to have separate locations for headquarters and branch plants?

**Q4** What name is given to the low-wage branches that result from a division of labour within tertiary industries such as banks?

ANSWERS

# the spatial separation of the low-skilled and high-skilled parts of a company

A1 The new international division of labour (NIDL)

A2 Footloose

A3 Falling transport costs; improved telecommunications networks; in high-income nations few places lack an electricity supply

A4 Back offices or call centres (e.g. many firms have call centres in India)

*examiner's* **note** In classical industrial location theory (e.g. Weber's model), a company seeks out a single least-cost location. With globalisation, the spatial division of labour allows firms to use geography to increase profits by seeking the least-cost location for different phases of the production process, all linked via modern telecommunication networks.

# Fordism

**Q1** After whom is Fordism named and why?

**Q2** Use of a c............ b............ or of an a............ l............ is usually central to the Fordist production process.

**Q3** How does this model of mass production in secondary industry help in turn to develop the tertiary sector?

**Q4** Why do Fordist industries find it difficult to adapt to rapidly changing consumer tastes and preferences?

ANSWERS

# the mass production of standardised manufactured goods

**A1** Henry Ford; he pioneered mass production of the motor car

**A2** Conveyor belt; assembly line

**A3** Workers are paid high wages to help boost productivity; this means more workers can afford to buy the goods they help to make

**A4** The machinery is inflexible and workers have rigidly defined tasks — it is therefore hard to change the design of the product

***examiner's* note** The link between production (workers making goods) and consumption (workers buying goods) is a vital aspect of economic growth. Workers in the nineteenth century were so exploited that they could afford to buy very little, which limited the expansion of domestic markets. Crucially, Ford changed this.

# Trading bloc

**Q1** What are NAFTA and EU abbreviations for?

**Q2** What are tariffs and import quota restrictions?

**Q3** How is free trade encouraged between the members of a trading bloc?

**Q4** How else does a trading bloc benefit its member states' industries?

**ANSWERS** ▶▶

**A1** North American Free Trade Association; European Union

**A2** A tariff is a fee charged to an importer of goods; a quota is a limit to the quantity of individual products that can be imported

**A3** By forming a customs union that removes internal tariffs while adopting a common external tariff

**A4** Increased economies of scale are achieved with a bigger market; specialisation occurs in areas of comparative advantage; greater protection exists from imports outside the bloc

*examiner's* **note** Trade blocs should not be treated as a homogenous group; some are purely economic entities with a common tariff, while others attempt political union. The European Union has moved beyond a common market towards full economic union with a common currency and some shared legislation.

# Economy of scale

**Q1** What is an internal economy of scale?

**Q2** What is an external economy of scale?

**Q3** By what other name is industrial clustering also known?

**Q4** A drinks manufacturer offers to sell a shop 100 cans for £20 or 200 for £30. There is a fixed delivery charge of £10. Bulk-buying 200 will allow what saving to be made per can?

ANSWERS

## the cost advantages gained by large-scale industrial production and selling

A1 A strategy that allows a firm, acting alone, to lower its unit costs, e.g. through bulk buying

A2 A joint strategy undertaken by several firms to lower unit costs by clustering together and sharing costs or by exchanging semi-finished products with one another

A3 Agglomeration

A4 $(£20 + £10)/100 = 30p$; $(£30 + £10)/200 = 20p$; 10p per can is saved

***examiner's* note** Economy of scale is also an important concept in relation to the location of retailing. Out-of-town retailers are able to bulk-buy from suppliers as they have much more space to stock products than they would have in a town centre, where land is more expensive and floor space restricted. Goods can then be sold for less because of the savings made through bulk-buying.

# Deindustrialisation

**Q1** What might be a physical cause of deindustrialisation?

**Q2** Suggest an economic cause of deindustrialisation.

**Q3** How might political factors contribute to this?

**Q4** What are the immediate economic and social consequences?

ANSWERS

## a sustained decline in industrial (especially manufacturing) employment and/or output

A1 Exhaustion of raw materials, or cheaper reserves found elsewhere; silting-up of a river relied on for transport

A2 Rising labour costs or cheaper labour found elsewhere; sales fall due to the saturation of markets; new inventions making a product obsolete

A3 Final removal of state support for struggling industries; changes in domestic policy (e.g. the end of a phase of council-house or motorway building devastates the supply industries)

A4 Unemployment, rising crime and social disorder

***examiner's* note** Deindustrialisation can depress one region while the nation as a whole performs well because of growth in other sectors in other regions. Although the short-term costs are high, the long-term benefits may be good, especially for the environment.

 **ANSWERS**

# Economic development

**Q1** What is the difference between gross national product (GNP) and gross domestic product (GDP)?

**Q2** Is GNP per capita or GDP per capita the preferred measure of economic development? Why?

**Q3** What other economic indicators of development exist?

**Q4** Why might estimates of national wealth give a misleading idea of the *typical* quality of life?

ANSWERS

## an increase in average levels of wealth and prosperity within a region

A1 GNP is economic output of all a nation's firms, including overseas operations; GDP is output produced within a nation's borders

A2 GDP. It is a better indicator of levels of local wealth creation.

A3 Gross domestic income (GDI); levels of car ownership; unemployment levels; purchasing power parity (an adjusted form of GDP that looks at ability to buy a 'basket' of goods at market prices)

A4 Wealth might all belong to an elite; figures do not include informal (unofficial) work or give financial value to subsistence farming

**examiner's note** Indicators of economic development do not give a reliable estimate of typical quality of life. In addition to the mechanical problems of using measures such as GDP, their usage implies that getting richer means better quality of life. However, studies suggest levels of wealth and happiness do not always correlate.

# Social development

**Q1** Why is social development likely to correlate with economic development?

**Q2** The human development index (HDI) combines social and economic indicators of development. Name its three ingredients.

**Q3** Why might HDI comparisons between countries be flawed?

**Q4** Why is it hard to establish a universally valued measure of social development?

**ANSWERS** ▶▶

## an estimate of qualify of life based on health, education and welfare

**A1** The scale and sophistication of health, education and other forms of welfare provision all depend upon a country's economy

**A2** Life expectancy; adult literacy rates; purchasing power parity (a modified form of GDP per capita)

**A3** Different countries may have different standards for measuring indicators such as literacy; some might not even collect data

**A4** Different societies have different values. A low birth rate might not signify advancement to someone who is opposed to contraception.

***examiner's* note** Development is a complex idea. Its meaning reflects a society's belief system and therefore changes as social attitudes shift. For instance, women lacked rights in the nineteenth century, yet Victorian society considered itself highly developed.

 **ANSWERS**

# Informal sector

**Q1** What term is given to work that is officially registered and declared?

**Q2** Which sector of industry contains the majority of informal work?

**Q3** What are the benefits of informal work for an LEDC government?

**Q4** What are the costs of informal work to an LEDC government?

ANSWERS

A1 Formal employment

A2 Tertiary (sales and services)

A3 The informal sector absorbs the unemployed, ensuring the
government does not have to provide benefits

A4 Workers put pressure on public services, such as roads and
healthcare, without contributing by paying taxes

*examiner's* **note** Informal work is not easily included in GNP or GDP figures,
which can mean that average per capita productivity is underestimated and that
assessments of levels of economic development are flawed. In some provinces of
India, as much as 80% of work is informal. The EU has a smaller informal sector
but estimates suggest it might still contain 20 million people.

# Debt crisis

**Q1** Who, other than commercial banks, lends money to nations?

**Q2** What is a structural adjustment programme (SAP)?

**Q3** What are the short-term social disadvantages of agreeing to structural adjustments?

**Q4** Where did the money come from that was loaned to many LEDCs by commercial banks in the 1970s?

ANSWERS

the inability of poor countries
that have borrowed money to
repay the interest on the loan

A1 The International Monetary Fund (IMF) and World Bank

A2 A series of reforms on which the IMF insists before making a loan, usually involving the abolition of barriers to foreign investment

A3 A nation may be asked to curb spending on public services such as health, education and water supplies

A4 Money ('petrodollars') invested by oil-producing countries such as Saudi Arabia, all of which made great profits during this decade

**examiner's note** Be able to evaluate the costs and benefits to a nation of agreeing to an SAP before receiving a loan. It is intended that further debt crises of the sort that occurred in 1982, when Mexico declared itself bankrupt, will be avoided through the use of SAPs. However, there are environmental and social risks associated with opening borders to foreign investors.

 **ANSWERS**

# Aid

**Q1** What is aid given by one country to another called?
And when there are several donors?

**Q2** Why do some countries receive more aid than others?

**Q3** Why might aid be withheld from a needy country with a
corrupt government?

**Q4** What is tied aid? Why is it sometimes criticised?

ANSWERS

## money, food or goods given by one country (or organisation) to another

A1 Bilateral; multilateral

A2 Historical ties with rich donors (ex-colonies); culture or religion may be shared with rich donors; strategic (military) reasons for the donor's gift

A3 Aid might not reach the people who need it. Alternatively, distributing the aid might boost the government's popularity.

A4 The recipient must spend the money on goods produced by the donor; cheaper goods may be available elsewhere

*examiner's* **note** Cheaply bought Ethiopian coffee is widely drunk in the UK yet Ethiopia is also a major recipient of aid from UK charities. Might it be better to just pay more to the coffee farmers? Development agencies that use the slogan 'fair trade not aid' believe so.

# Trade

**Q1** What name is given to an economic exchange that occurs without any interruption or barriers?

**Q2** What are barriers to trade called? How do they differ for primary and secondary goods?

**Q3** What does the law of comparative advantage state?

**Q4** What name is given to trade that guarantees LEDC farmers a fair price for their produce?

**ANSWERS** 》

# the flow of goods or services from producers to consumers

A1 Free trade

A2 Tariffs; there are fewer restrictions for most manufactured goods

A3 Regions should specialise in producing those products for which they have the greatest cost advantage over others, due to factors of production such as resource endowments or skills

A4 Fair trade

*examiner's* **note** Countries that move beyond trading primary products to export-oriented manufacturing can develop rapidly. This is certainly true of newly industrialised countries (NICs) such as the Asian Tigers (Hong Kong, South Korea, Singapore and Taiwan) and more recently China and Indonesia.

# Dependency

**Q1** In the past, a country that was conquered by an invading power and added to its empire became a c................

**Q2** Why has dependency persisted beyond the end of empires?

**Q3** According to dependency theory, why are LEDCs that export raw materials and import manufactured goods at a disadvantage?

**Q4** Which writer is usually associated with dependency theory?

ANSWERS ▶▶

A1 Colony

A2 It is hard to break away from the import–export trade
relationships established under colonialism once they are
established

A3 Manufacturing produces high value-added goods while raw material
prices are relatively much lower (with a few exceptions such as
oil). LEDCs may be left with a trade deficit and large debts.

A4 Gunder Frank (1967)

***examiner's* note** Dependency theory is important because it teaches us to
consider that poverty might not be the fault of an individual state but produced
by the historical relationships between countries. The rich get richer because
they have the power to maintain existing trade relationships with the poor.
There is no level playing field.

# Colonialism

**Q1** Colonialism is the first phase of modern g............. and began in which century?

**Q2** Which European countries had the largest empires?

**Q3** When did India gain independence?

**Q4** According to critics of globalisation, what has colonialism been replaced by?

**ANSWERS**

A1 Globalisation; fifteenth century

A2 Spain, Portugal, Britain, France, Holland, Belgium, Germany

A3 1947

A4 Neocolonialism (poor countries are still controlled by rich
countries but through trade rules and other indirect means)

*examiner's* **note** The consequences of colonialism continue to this day.
Migrant labour flows, aid donations and trade relationships often reflect past
histories. For instance, the UK has much stronger links with India and Jamaica
than with Algeria (which was a French colony). Equally, armed conflicts in LEDCs
such as Rwanda frequently have their origins in the artificial borders created by
colonialism and the power vacuum left by decolonisation.

# Underdevelopment theory

**Q1** Underdevelopment theory investigates the claim that 'the rich get ............... while the poor get ...............'.

**Q2** Why has the price paid to world coffee producers fallen?

**Q3** Why is mortality increasing in some of the world's poorest countries, such as Sierra Leone?

**Q4** What percentage of the world's poorest people earns the same amount of money as the richest 1%?

ANSWERS

**A1** Richer; poorer

**A2** Overproduction has flooded world markets, as more subsistence farmers have turned to cash-cropping

**A3** Civil war; famine may be linked to population growth; falling prices for exports; desertification; HIV/AIDS

**A4** 57%. The richest 50 million earn the same as the poorest 2.7 billion, according to the World Bank.

***examiner's* note** Underdeveloped nations are linked with developed nations in a system of economic exchanges, or flows, of raw materials, manufactured goods and labour. Some geographers claim these flows leave poor countries worse-off than they would otherwise be, hence the phrase 'the development of underdevelopment'.

# Rostow's model

**Q1** What is take-off?

**Q2** What are the preconditions for take-off?

**Q3** Name the two stages that follow take-off.

**Q4** Why might the arrival of transnational corporations (TNCs) in an LEDC not contribute to take-off?

ANSWERS

**A1** Self-sustaining growth based upon a multiplier effect, usually driven by export-orientated manufacturing

**A2** Pioneering of new industrial techniques and infrastructure growth

**A3** • The drive to maturity
  • The age of high mass consumption

**A4** The profits might be repatriated to the TNC's nation of origin; under such conditions, truly sustainable economic growth might not occur

***examiner's* note** The reason why some countries have achieved industrial take-off and not others is a controversial topic. The sociologist Max Weber, for instance, believed that the 'work ethic' of Protestant Christianity aided England's early industrial revolution. Similarly, it is often argued that the Asian Tigers have succeeded where others have failed because of their own superior 'work ethic'. How convincing is this?

# Cumulative causation

**Q1** Core growth begins in areas that possess n............... a............... of some sort, such as good climate or soils.

**Q2** Self-sustaining economic growth depends upon the multiplier effect. Describe how this works.

**Q3** If the core experiences 'virtuous growth circles', what does the periphery experience?

**Q4** Which writer is often associated with cumulative causation?

ANSWERS ▶▶

A1 Natural advantages

A2 Successive new layers of investment and migration are attracted to the core, drawn by ever-increasing opportunities both to make and to sell goods as the market expands

A3 Vicious growth circles or downward spirals

A4 Myrdal (1957); also Friedmann (1966) and Hirschman (1958)

***examiner's* note** Opinions differ on whether inequalities will persist or diminish over time. Myrdal believed inequality would, on balance, persist (peripheral regions may receive some benefits such as government aid, but these are not enough to offset continuing backwash of resources to the core). However, Friedmann believed that real wealth and opportunity would be dispersed to the periphery over time.

# Core and periphery

**Q1** Suggest three different scales of geography at which core–periphery patterns can be seen.

**Q2** What non-economic functions are associated with core regions?

**Q3** Flows to the core are called b............., while those to the periphery are called s............. e.............

**Q4** What name is given to parts of the periphery that grow?

ANSWERS

## two regions with uneven levels of growth, linked by flows of migrants, trade and investment

**A1** Choose from: national (e.g. the north–south divide in the UK); international (the EU has its own core); global (with MEDCs serving as a global core); local (a town serves as a core to a rural periphery)

**A2** Political (government); cultural (media and the arts); social (universities)

**A3** Backwash; spread effects (also known as trickle-down)

**A4** Upward transitional areas or growth poles

***examiner's* note** It might be argued that the core–periphery system benefits all, as peripheral areas gain indirectly from innovations developed in the core and directly from aid. Be able to debate this viewpoint critically using detailed case studies, preferably one LEDC and one MEDC.

# Growth pole

**Q1** What name is given to the cost advantages gained by industries that have clustered together?

**Q2** For a growth pole to develop fully, what must a government provide?

**Q3** What is a technopole?

**Q4** What name is given to a growth pole that stretches along a major transport route, such as the M4?

**ANSWERS**

# a cluster of industrial expansion in a peripheral area rather than a core region

**A1** Agglomeration economy (or economy of scale)

**A2** Good transport and communications infrastructure; education

**A3** A growth pole that has developed around quaternary industries (such as computer hardware and software design)

**A4** Growth corridor

*examiner's* **note** Growth poles do not always maintain growth. For instance, success stories in Scotland based around North Sea oil or the expansion of tourism have faltered. Be able to evaluate the long-term success of growth pole policies you have studied (typically in Italy, Brazil or France). A planned growth pole that fails to achieve sustainable growth is sometimes labelled a 'cathedral in the desert'.

# Settlement pattern

**Q1** Where do physical factors give rise to linear patterns?

**Q2** Which physical factors encourage nucleation?

**Q3** How do political factors influence the dispersal of settlements?

**Q4** Which analytical technique is used to quantify the degree of clustering or dispersion in a group of settlements?

ANSWERS

## the way in which a group of settlements are positioned in relation to each another

A1 At the base of chalk slopes ('springline settlements'); along valley floors; on raised beaches in Scotland; along coastlines

A2 Clustering often occurs in lowland areas with fertile (non-acidic) soils, a longer growing season and good water supply

A3 Regional policies can aid and encourage dispersion, especially through New Town programmes (as in the UK or Egypt)

A4 Nearest neighbour analysis

*examiner's* **note** Much of what is written here is also applicable to the morphology (form) of individual settlements, which can be described as linear or nucleated. However, additional factors can influence individual settlement forms, such as the survival of a historic feature (e.g. a church or village green), planning controls and historical influences, such as strip farming (which generates linear housing patterns).

# Site and situation

**Q1** Define site.

**Q2** What physical factors affect choice of a site?

**Q3** Define situation.

**Q4** Give an example of a situation that favours trade.

ANSWERS

# the factors that explain the location of a settlement

A1 The land a settlement is built on

A2 Water supply; relief; soils; shelter; resources

A3 The location of a settlement in relation to other settlements and external resources

A4 Choose from: a bridging point or gap in hills along a trade route; an estuary or harbour that favours trade with other regions; proximity to main transport routes

***examiner's* note** Some of these factors are dynamic and could change over time as a result of environmental or political changes. For instance, over the last 50 years, Liverpool's situation has changed for the worse as Britain's trade links with America have weakened and those with Europe have grown (situated on the west coast, Liverpool's growth was originally based on trade with the Americas).

# Settlement hierarchy

**Q1** Name the four commonly identified levels of settlement in a regional hierarchy.

**Q2** State four characteristics of high-order settlements.

**Q3** Why are some settlements hard to place within a hierarchy?

**Q4** Why might a change occur to a settlement's position within a regional or national hierarchy?

ANSWERS

## the grouping of settlements according to population size and number of central-place services

A1 Hamlets; villages; towns; cities

A2 Large population; many high-order services; relatively few such settlements exist; they are spaced far apart

A3 Commuting towns and mining towns have large populations but few services; the opposite might be true for tourist and university towns

A4 Decline of its services or industries (deindustrialisation); growth of new services or industries; direct government influence (e.g. awarding of city status); indirect government influence (e.g. the result of transport policies)

***examiner's* note** On some exam specifications, this topic is taught by emphasising the concept of *centrality*. The higher a settlement is placed in a hierarchy, the greater its degree of centrality.

# Threshold and range

**Q1** Define threshold.

**Q2** Define range.

**Q3** Why are low-order services able to maintain a profit despite having only a small customer base?

**Q4** Why might identical services located in different socio-economic neighbourhoods not have the same threshold population?

ANSWERS 》

## concepts that help explain the degree of centrality of a settlement and the level of services it provides

A1 The minimum number of customers that make a business profitable

A2 The maximum distance people will travel for a service

A3 Although the customers are buying low-cost items, they do so on an everyday basis, thereby generating sufficient profits

A4 A supermarket near a council estate will cater mostly for people on low incomes; therefore, more customers are needed to maintain a profit than in a gentrified area where incomes are higher

***examiner's* note** Modern trends in retailing sometimes make the concept of range hard to apply. Increased personal mobility has fostered the growth of out-of-town stores, which sell low-range items like milk and bread to people who have actually travelled a great distance. More recently, internet shopping has begun to develop, further challenging our understanding of the concept of range.

 **ANSWERS**

# Sphere of influence

**Q1** What is the relationship between the range of a settlement and its sphere of influence?

**Q2** How do we distinguish between a primary (intensive) and secondary (extensive) sphere of influence?

**Q3** Why are spheres of influence rarely circular?

**Q4** If a settlement serves a large number of smaller centres within its sphere of influence, it is said to display a high level of what?

**ANSWERS**

## the area surrounding a settlement that is served by the central-place services found there

A1 Range is the maximum distance people will travel for a settlement's services. It is the radius of the sphere of influence (SoI).

A2 A small primary SoI exists for low-order goods, such as newspapers, that some surrounding villages can provide for themselves. A much larger secondary SoI exists for specialist items, such as furniture.

A3 They are truncated by physical features (rivers or coastlines) and administrative boundaries (for schools and hospitals)

A4 Centrality

***examiner's* note** The size of the SoI is influenced by the characteristics of the surrounding area. The threshold of high-order central-place services can be met by a small SoI if the region has a high population density or is home to particularly affluent people. 'Urban field' and 'hinterland' are alternate names for SoI.

# Breakpoint

**Q1** Calculate $D_{AB} \sqrt{[1 + P_A/P_B]}$ where $D_{AB}$ (distance between settlements A and B) is 20 km and $P_A$ and $P_B$ (populations of towns A and B) are 50 000 and 20 000. What does the result tell us?

**Q2** Why might people not visit their nearest high-order settlement when buying an item such as shoes?

**Q3** Why is population a poor measure of a town's attractiveness?

**Q4** Why might a town's retail attractiveness change over time?

ANSWERS

# where the market areas
# of two settlements meet

A1 $20 \sqrt{[1 + \sqrt{50\,000/20\,000}]} = 7.75$ km; this means that the breakpoint is 7.75 km from settlement B

A2 They may have personal reasons to go elsewhere; shoes may be sold there but the range might be limited or else they are of poor quality

A3 Some settlements, such as commuting villages, may have a large population but offer relatively few services

A4 Retail services might decentralise to an out-of-town site

**examiner's note** Reilly's breakpoint model is driven by an assumption that people always act in a rational and predictable way, attempting to minimise economic costs. However, the psychology of decision-making is in fact very complex. For instance, no model can account for the fact that some people may travel further than their nearest newsagent for a paper because they find the shopkeeper disagreeable.

# Urban

**Q1** What three criteria can be used to define urban areas?

**Q2** What proportion of the world's population lives in urban areas? What is the figure for the UK?

**Q3** What name is given to the area of countryside that falls under the economic, social and political influence of an urban settlement?

**Q4** What does the phrase 'rural–urban continuum' tell us?

ANSWERS

A1 Settlement population size (10 000 in England and Wales); population density (typically at least 100 people per km$^2$); function (e.g. the presence of high-order retailing or manufacturing industries)

A2 One half; in the UK it is around 79%

A3 Sphere of influence (or urban field or hinterland)

A4 There is no clear dividing line between rural and urban land uses

*examiner's* **note** Although 10 000 people is the normal benchmark, government agencies in England and Wales sometimes include settlements with as few as 1000 people in their urban statistics. This makes an additional 5.1 million people 'urban', raising the national urban population to 90%.

# City

**Q1** What is a world (or global) city?

**Q2** What are the functions of a pre-industrial city?

**Q3** What types of employment dominate in a post-industrial city?

**Q4** What is a megacity?

ANSWERS

## a settlement with higher-order functions and a larger population than are found in a town

A1  A city in which a disproportionate part of the world's most important business is conducted, e.g. London, Tokyo and New York

A2  Administration, religion, trade and military

A3  Retail, leisure services and quaternary sector work

A4  A city with a population of 10 million or more

*examiner's* **note** As they industrialise, cities draw upon surrounding areas for their manufacturing workforce. A shift usually occurs from 'city-serving' to 'city-forming' activities. However, this is not always the case: 'urbanisation without industrialisation' has occurred in parts of Africa and Asia. High rates of natural increase here are not matched by rates of industrial growth. This causes chronic underemployment.

# Megacity

**Q1** What is the world's largest megacity?

**Q2** Name Africa's two largest megacities.

**Q3** Why might the population statistics used to count the population of a megacity be unreliable?

**Q4** Why are the fastest-growing megacities at risk of becoming unsustainable?

ANSWERS

# a city or urban area with more than 10 million residents

A1 Tokyo

A2 Lagos and Cairo

A3 Rapid rates of migration into the city mean that data are quickly out of date; slum settlements are difficult to survey for census purposes

A4 The rate of arrival of new migrants may be so great that it outpaces improvements being made to housing, sanitation and transport

***examiner's* note** Do not confuse the term 'megacity' with 'world city'. A megacity is defined simply in terms of the number of residents living there, whereas a world city is a settlement that exerts major global political and economic power. Thus, New York is a megacity and a world city; Paris is a world city but not a megacity.

# Urbanisation

**Q1** Name two demographic causes of urban population growth.

**Q2** How might urbanisation be measured other than by population growth?

**Q3** What is the key 'pull' factor that draws people to cities?

**Q4** When might urbanisation occur without industrialisation?

ANSWERS ▶▶

A1 Natural increase; migration

A2 Growth in city size; growth in industrial employment levels; addition of new higher-order functions; changing social attitudes; growth of democracy often accompanies urban growth

A3 Employment, in both the formal and informal sectors

A4 Pre-industrial cities often have specialised functions (e.g. religion or education); refugees from war, floods or famine can also aid growth

*examiner's* **note** This is the most significant process encountered in contemporary human geography. The number of people living in cities has grown by 2.1 billion worldwide since 1950. Although most MEDC cities are no longer growing, there are important anomalies such as Tokyo and Los Angeles, which you should investigate.

# Land-use model

**Q1** (a) Which writer is associated with the use of ring models?
(b) Which writer is remembered for his sector model?

**Q2** Why do land-use sectors develop?

**Q3** What is the great advantage of Mann's model (1965)?

**Q4** Why might a city have multiple nuclei (more than one central business district)?

ANSWERS

## a simplified illustration of the pattern of residential, industrial and commercial land use in an urban area

A1 (a) Burgess     (b) Hoyt

A2 Industry develops along transport lines and rivers; better housing avoids industry; raised river terraces might attract high-class housing

A3 It combines rings (echoing historical growth patterns) and sectors (which are related to prevailing wind patterns)

A4 City growth can envelop other towns (as London absorbed Camden); it might have been planned that way

***examiner's note*** Historic background to a settlement will determine which model is the best fit. In the UK, old market towns that have expanded steadily over centuries often display rings (e.g. Salisbury); rapid-growth industrial towns and planned settlements (e.g. Milton Keynes) might have been designed on a sectoral or multiple-nuclei basis. No single model can be expected to serve in all cases.

# Concentric urban growth

**Q1** Why do cities tend to expand outwards in concentric growth models?

**Q2** Why did the rate of outward expansion increase in American and British cities during the twentieth century?

**Q3** Why is the central business district (CBD) found in the middle of cities?

**Q4** What sort of land use surrounds the CBD in MEDC cities that have developed a concentric pattern?

ANSWERS

# a series of circular zones of differing land use that spread outwards from a town or city centre

A1  New migrants arrive looking for cheap accommodation near the city centre; existing residents in turn move further out

A2  The introduction of trains and electric trams extended work journeys; rising wages met these new commuting costs

A3  Profits are maximised there because of their heightened accessibility and this encourages high bidding from retailers

A4  The zone of transition (or inner city): an area of mixed land use including light industry, older housing and car parks

*examiner's* **note** In MEDC cities, the best-quality housing is often found in the outermost ring. Cheaper land (measured in £/m²) allows for large detached properties to be built. However, in LEDC cities, the pattern is often reversed, with the final ring consisting of low-quality shanty houses built on unoccupied land.

# Urban physical influences

**Q1** How do prevailing winds affect land use in many British cities?

**Q2** What types of land use are associated with river floodplains?

**Q3** Why did areas on higher ground often generate high land values in British cities of the nineteenth century?

**Q4** What word best describes the survival of a mining town even after its physical resources have been exhausted?

ANSWERS ▶▶

# how the physical environment affects the site, size, shape and zoning of urban areas

A1 Westerly winds blow city-centre pollution eastwards; the 'west end' originally attracted the rich, leaving the 'east end' to the poor

A2 Industry (flat land, water supply and transport); poorer housing (in the absence of flood defences); high-class housing (with flood defences); urban nature reserves (after river restoration schemes)

A3 Cleaner air and water (lower cholera risk); aesthetic appeal of the view

A4 Inertia

*examiner's* **note** The question 'how does the physical environment influence the character of urban areas?' is open to many interpretations, such as the effects on site, size, shape or zoning of the settlement. You could even consider how famous rivers or other landscape features appear in the everyday culture of cities like Liverpool and London (celebrated in song, poetry, painting, as well as street and building names).

# Urban functions

**Q1** What are the three main functions of urban areas?

**Q2** What is the economic theory that explains the distribution of these three main land uses?

**Q3** Why are some areas of urban land not dedicated to these functions?

**Q4** What change of function is occurring in many British inner cities? Why?

ANSWERS ▶▶

# broad groupings of activities occurring in a town or city

A1 Residential; industrial; commercial (retail and offices)

A2 Bid–rent theory

A3 Planning laws might preserve parkland (as recreation for residents and workers); some land may be unsafe (e.g. floodplains)

A4 A shift from industrial to residential functions. The closure or relocation of traditional industries is due to foreign competition, while rising incomes allow more homeowners to afford expensive luxury apartments in inner-city converted warehouses and factories.

***examiner's* note** 'Function' does not always have the same meaning as 'land use'. For instance, if a furniture store is replaced by a clothes store, then there has been no change in function as both are types of retailing. However, were the store to be converted to residential flats, then a functional change would have occurred.

# Urban industries

**Q1** Why are centres of newly industrialised cities (including European cities in the 1800s) usually dominated by large industries?

**Q2** Most urban industry has decentralised, yet breweries can still be found near the centre of some European cities. Why?

**Q3** What kinds of small-scale manufacturing still survive in the centres of many European or American cities?

**Q4** What are the attractions of edge-of-city industrial estates for modern industry in high-income nations?

ANSWERS ▶▶

## market-orientated or labour-intensive industries that maximise profits by locating in towns and cities

**A1** Industries develop where resources are found or transport is good. Cities then grow around them as labour migrants arrive.

**A2** They are 'weight-gaining' industries — most of the product is simply water. Producing drinks near their market reduces transport costs.

**A3** Luxury items such as fashion garments or handmade furniture and ceramics. Small-batch, flexible production occurs in 'workshop' units and the goods are sold to nearby department stores or boutiques.

**A4** Cheap land; room for expansion; easy access to motorways

***examiner's* note** Generally, large-output factory operations have abandoned MEDC cities and relocated in countries where labour is cheaper. Cities in China now house the production plants and labour force for giant multinational corporations such as Sony or Gap.

 **ANSWERS**

# Urban population density

**Q1** Where is population density highest in MEDC cities?

**Q2** Why is this the case?

**Q3** Why might population densities begin to rise as you approach the edge of towns and cities in MEDCs?

**Q4** Why, contrary to urban models, can housing often be found in the CBD?

ANSWERS

## the number of people per square kilometre within an urban area

A1  The inner city, surrounding the CBD

A2  High land values encourage the conversion of single-occupier buildings into flats; a lack of gardens and parking spaces further contributes to the high density of housing

A3  Presence of post-war housing estates; countryside views drive land prices higher, resulting in higher building densities

A4  Upper storeys of tall buildings may be residential; council housing is provided in all city boroughs, even in Westminster (central London)

***examiner's* note** Be aware of how housing types vary in different areas of the city. Typically, inner-city Victorian housing is terraced in the UK. Suburban housing is semi-detached or detached, reflecting lower land costs per unit area. This allows bigger houses to be bought at a lower cost than similar-sized properties near the city centre. Suburban plots of land in US cities can be very large.

 **ANSWERS**

# Urban services

**Q1** What are high-order services?

**Q2** What are low-order services?

**Q3** How are low-order services distributed in urban areas?

**Q4** What recent locational trends do you associate with high-order services?

ANSWERS ▶▶

## shops and other services that provide for urban populations and people in surrounding settlements

A1 Providers of higher-cost products/services that are bought or used infrequently (e.g. a furniture store or a dentist). Customers are prepared to travel long distances for them.

A2 Providers of lower-cost, 'everyday' products (e.g. a newsagent). Customers will not travel long distances for them.

A3 They are regularly spaced in residential neighbourhoods

A4 Decentralisation from the CBD towards suburban retail parks

*examiner's* **note** Be aware that the period of rapid expansion for out-of-town retailing is now over. The growing refusal of government to grant permission for new green-belt developments is turning retailers' attention back towards city centres. Gentrification (reurbanisation) is also occurring, with large numbers of affluent people moving into inner cities. UK supermarkets are now starting to provide these areas with 'metro' style outlets.

# Central business district (CBD)

**Q1** What is functional zoning? Why does it occur?

**Q2** Why do service providers such as solicitors and dentists often only occupy higher floors?

**Q3** Why have some CBDs experienced a relative decline in trade?

**Q4** How might city-centre retailing be revived?

ANSWERS

# the nucleus of an urban area, containing the main concentration of shops and offices

A1 The clustering of similar services (e.g. a street full of antique shops). By fostering an area's reputation for a particular service, trade is greatly increased to the point where profits increase for all retailers.

A2 Clients are seen by appointment. They do not rely on casual trade in the way that ground-floor retailers do (this is vertical zoning).

A3 Because of competition from out-of-town retailers

A4 By improving the shopping environment through a combination of all-weather malls, pedestrianised streets, park-and-ride schemes and CCTV video cameras (to reduce crime risk)

***examiner's* note** One way to regenerate a CBD might be to develop different types of consumer service. Cultural facilities such as museums and art galleries could be established, while bars and restaurants might replace shops. This is called urban rebranding.

 **(73)** **ANSWERS**

# Bid–rent theory

**Q1** In a free market, who obtains the use of a piece of land?

**Q2** What dictates the value of a piece of land?

**Q3** Why is accessibility important for high-order retailers?

**Q4** What is the point of highest land value called? Where is it found?

ANSWERS ▶▶

## an explanation of how free-market economic forces generate urban land-use patterns

A1 The highest bidder

A2 Retailers calculate the profit that can be made there; home-owners and industries consider the travel costs associated with use of the site and adjust their bid accordingly

A3 Accessible sites have high pedestrian flows that increase levels of casual custom and maximise profits

A4 Peak land value intersection (PLVI); usually at the centre of the CBD

***examiner's* note** Secondary land value peaks occur when accessibility is good (where arterial and ring roads meet). Housing bids are increased by good schools and parks but lowered by proximity to industry. Not all urban patterns are a product of bid–rent processes. Planning laws ensure the preservation of parkland and listed buildings and may enforce strict zoning of land uses.

 **ANSWERS**

# Out-of-town retail

**Q1** What costs might prompt a retailer to leave the CBD?

**Q2** What are the benefits of relocating to the edges of a settlement?

**Q3** Why is this only a relatively recent phenomenon (over the last 40 years)?

**Q4** Distinguish between hypermarkets and retail shopping centres.

ANSWERS

## retailing that has decentralised from the CBD to accessible parts of the rural–urban fringe

A1 High land prices in town centres; commuting costs for staff

A2 Cheap land; room for expansion and car parking; storage space allows for bulk-buying, so that economies of scale can be achieved

A3 Incomes used to be lower (creating less demand for goods); growth of road networks and car ownership have improved suburban access in many nations since the mid-twentieth century

A4 Hypermarkets are very large branches of a retail chain, usually found at the edge of a city in retail parks. Retail shopping centres, such as Bluewater (Kent, UK), are large structures, purpose-built to house many retailers and are often located beyond the city edge.

***examiner's* note** Be able to evaluate carefully the impact of this trend. Consider the advantages and disadvantages of both traditional CBDs and the new areas of expansion. Impacts should cover economic, social and environmental aspects.

 **ANSWERS**

# Inner-city decline

**Q1** How did industrial changes contribute to the decline of inner-city areas in MEDCs after the 1960s?

**Q2** How has urban–rural migration contributed to these problems?

**Q3** What designation was given to particularly hard-hit areas of UK cities during the 1980s in order to assist their survival and renovation?

**Q4** Which inner-city problems occur independently of long-term decline?

**ANSWERS**

## increased deprivation in poorer areas bordering the central business district

A1 The greatest job losses were found in these areas when traditional industries fell into decline during the 1970s

A2 The decentralisation of affluent people to suburbs and villages has left some areas with income levels well below the national average. This makes it harder to raise taxes to provide good local services.

A3 Enterprise zones

A4 Traffic congestion and pollution; ageing housing in need of modernisation; relative lack of green spaces

***examiner's* note** Inner-city problems are part of a much wider process of uneven development occurring in Europe and the USA since the 1960s. High levels of growth have occurred in services and quaternary industries, but often only in suburban and fringe areas. Dereliction in inner cities deters new investment, leaving pockets of poverty in cities such as Baltimore (USA) and Sheffield (UK).

# Cycle of poverty

**Q1** How does a cycle of poverty operate?

**Q2** Why have some European and US cities suffered greater poverty than others in recent decades?

**Q3** What term is used to describe an area suffering from a series of social, economic and environmental deprivations?

**Q4** Apart from inner cities, where else in MEDCs might communities experiencing severe deprivation be found?

ANSWERS

## self-perpetuating poverty transmitted between generations of families in deprived areas

A1 Unemployment and high crime rates cause staffing problems for local services, including schools. Local shops close as incomes fall. All of this damages job prospects for the next generation.

A2 Places dominated by a single industry, such as coal or steel, suffered the worst rises in long-term unemployment in the 1970s and 1980s

A3 Multiple deprivation

A4 Suburban (social housing) estates; declining rural villages

*examiner's* **note** A cycle of poverty is an example of a negative multiplier effect, where the collapse of one industry leads to many more redundancies in supply industries and also in services that rely upon local wages. For every job lost in London's docklands during the 1970s, another three were lost in supply and service industries.

**(77) ANSWERS**

# Urban regeneration

**Q1** Why did widespread building work take place in British cities during the 1950s and 1960s?

**Q2** Why did attention shift away from housing and towards economic and social conditions in MEDC cities during the 1970s and 1980s?

**Q3** What are enterprise zones (introduced to the UK in 1981)?

**Q4** Older cities might struggle to achieve new investment because of their poor image. How might this be changed?

ANSWERS ▶▶

# government-led efforts to redevelop older urban neighbourhoods

A1 To replace buildings damaged in the 1939–45 war; to replace Victorian slum housing that lacked indoor toilets

A2 Deindustrialisation was beginning to harm communities; immigration was bringing new challenges

A3 Small areas of high unemployment where a range of incentives are made available for a ten-year period to attract new investment

A4 Via prestige projects such as new sports stadiums; by awarding a title such as 'City of Culture', thus rebranding the area

***examiner's* note** Regeneration is increasingly seen as an opportunity to introduce new sustainability measures. New housing projects can be designated 'carbon-neutral' if green designs are introduced.

# Gentrification

**Q1** What name is given to the effect that gentrification has on many MEDC cities?

**Q2** Why have an increasing number of middle-class people been 'pulled' towards inner urban areas in recent years?

**Q3** In what ways might this movement be age-selective?

**Q4** Why does gentrification often involve a change in function for inner urban areas?

ANSWERS

## movement of affluent people into previously devalued neighbourhoods, notably in inner cities

A1 Reurbanisation

A2 Easy access to work in city centre; accessibility to night-clubs, restaurants and theatres; perceived charm of older housing

A3 Young, affluent adults of pre-child and child-bearing ages are most commonly involved. Those of child-*rearing* ages may later relocate to suburban or fringe areas where larger houses are found.

A4 Industrial buildings and warehouses that have fallen out of use because of deindustrialisation are converted into modern housing units

***examiner's* note** Gentrification happens while counterurbanisation is also occurring (they usually involve slightly different age groups). However, in recent years, the net balance between the two has shifted. For instance, in some major cities, more people are now arriving than are leaving, causing population growth for the first time in decades.

 **ANSWERS**

# Ethnic village

**Q1** What is an ethnic group?

**Q2** What are the three largest ethnic minority groups in England and Wales (as shown by the UK National Census)?

**Q3** Why might ethnic groups choose to become segregated from the general population?

**Q4** What external constraints might force ethnic groups to become segregated in ghettos?

ANSWERS

## part of an urban area with a higher-than-average proportion of members of one ethnic group

A1 A group of people whose race, religion, language or country of birth differs from the majority of the population

A2 People of Indian (2%), Pakistani (1.4%) and Irish (1.2%) descent

A3 To be close to a place of worship; preservation of cultural identity; to achieve political representation by voting for group members in local elections (Harlem had the first black mayor in the USA)

A4 To avoid hostility and racism; discrimination in employment might lower wages, limiting ability to buy property in other areas

***examiner's* note** All large cities, especially ports with a long history of trade, tend to exhibit a mosaic of ethnic villages. The landscape evidence for this includes places of worship (mosques or synagogues mix with churches along London's skyline), as well as specialist services, retailers and restaurants.

# Shanty towns

**Q1** The world's population is 6.8 billion people. Approximately how many of these people live in shanty towns?

**Q2** What is the difference between squatter settlements and spontaneous settlements?

**Q3** Where are shanty towns located?

**Q4** How might conditions be improved?

ANSWERS ))

## areas of poorly built, low-cost and often illegal housing found in and around cities in LEDCs

A1 Around 1 billion

A2 Squatter settlements, although illegal, may have been planned by their inhabitants and possess basic infrastructure; spontaneous settlements lack infrastructure and are entirely unplanned

A3 On the edge of cities or wherever land is not used (because of flood or landslip risk); centres of employment also attract squatters

A4 If governments grant legal land rights to home-builders and provide infrastructure, then self-help improvements are encouraged

***examiner's* note** Be careful not to focus entirely upon the negative aspects of shanty towns. They house a large labour force that can attract foreign transnational companies. This might lead, in time, to improved conditions as the nation industrialises. Equally, if a country lacks the resources for public housing projects, what other options exist?

# Suburbanisation

**Q1** Suburbanisation contributes to urban sprawl. What is this called if it occurs along a transport route?

**Q2** In the UK, suburbanisation began in the late 1800s. Why not before then?

**Q3** What social and environmental problems lead to some people migrating away from inner cities?

**Q4** What originally attracted city-dwellers to the suburbs?

ANSWERS

## the outward expansion of a settlement, as people and economic activity relocate near its edges

A1 Ribbon development

A2 Prior to that, there were no mass transport systems (London's first steam-powered tube train ran on the Metropolitan Line in 1863; electric trams and trains soon followed)

A3 Overcrowding; perceptions of violent crime and disorder (e.g. London's Brixton riots of 1981); pollution and smog; health concerns (fears of tuberculosis remained strong in Europe until the middle of the twentieth century)

A4 Cheaper land meant larger houses; the quality of newly built schools and surgeries was often better than in inner cities

***examiner's* note** New waves of migrants arrive in the centre as existing residents head for the edges in a city experiencing suburbanisation. The city grows both in size and numbers during this period. Do not confuse the term with counterurbanisation.

# New Town

**Q1** How may New Towns be recognised on a map?

**Q2** Describe the population structure of a recently built New Town.

**Q3** Which decades are particularly associated with New Town development in post-war Britain?

**Q4** What is an eco-town?

ANSWERS

## a planned, purpose-built and free-standing urban centre added to an existing settlement system

A1 Wide, curving streets laid out in a regular pattern; evidence of careful zoning of land uses

A2 Relatively youthful with a low proportion of pensioners (due to the selective in-migration of families with young children)

A3 Late 1940s through to the end of the 1960s

A4 A purpose-built, sustainable settlement that uses green technology to achieve carbon-neutral living

***examiner's* note** Both first-generation UK New Towns such as Stevenage (population: 81 000; designated: 1946) and second-generation ones such as Milton Keynes (population: 210 000; designated: 1967) were intended to be free-standing, self-sufficient settlements and not dormitory towns. Milton Keynes is the business base for 3500 firms, including high-profile overseas companies.

# Rural–urban fringe

**Q1** What uses are made of land at the rural–urban fringe?

**Q2** Why is planning permission for new building hard to obtain in fringe areas?

**Q3** What is ribbon development?

**Q4** How is land use different in fringe areas of LEDC cities?

ANSWERS

## a zone of change between the continuously built-up suburbs and the surrounding countryside

A1 Intensive agriculture; protected areas of woodland; leisure (golf courses, theme parks, retail parks); large-scale amenities (airports, sewage works, reservoirs)

A2 Much of the land is protected by green-belt legislation

A3 Urban growth that extends along major transport corridors into the rural–urban fringe

A4 Shanty towns develop at the rural–urban fringe, as migrants build their own houses on unoccupied sites

***examiner's* note** The characteristics of fringe areas vary considerably between cities and countries. In America, planning controls are often far less stringent that in Britain. As a consequence, new 'edge cities' ('exurbs') have been developing over the last 30 years on the outskirts of existing major settlements (e.g. Los Angeles).

# Rural

**Q1** Which three criteria can be used to define rural areas?

**Q2** Why are rural areas in LEDCs usually sending sites for migration, whereas in MEDCs they are increasingly receiving sites?

**Q3** What is the main sector of employment in rural Britain?

**Q4** What is meant by 'the rural idyll'?

ANSWERS ▶▶

## relating to the countryside and the life that is lived there

A1 Low population density; land uses including agriculture and forestry; low-order settlements and services

A2 LEDC governments struggle to provide basic services in rural areas and jobs there are largely farming-based. In MEDCs, essential services and employment possibilities are now available in rural areas.

A3 Tertiary work (retail, services and tourism)

A4 A romantic perception (often held by city-dwellers) of the countryside being free of danger, pollution or crime

*examiner's* **note** Rural Britain is a working countryside, although representations of rural areas often do not show this. Even many so-called wilderness areas contain indigenous people. Rural policy must always address the needs of these working rural people, while still trying to safeguard the natural environment.

**(85) ANSWERS**

# Rural functions

**Q1** What proportion of land in the UK is used for agriculture?

**Q2** Name four non-agricultural rural functions.

**Q3** What are National Parks and when were they established in the UK?

**Q4** Which UK government agency is responsible for forest policy?

ANSWERS

# activities occurring in the countryside

A1 73% (a further 11% is forest)

A2 Choose from: residential; tourism; mining; service industries (call centres and 'back offices'); forestry; out-of-town retail parks; water supply (reservoirs); nature reserves

A3 Areas of great natural beauty where any new development is strictly controlled; they were established in the UK in 1949

A4 The Forestry Commission

*examiner's* **note** Rural functions differ between areas, as do levels of conflict over land use. A proposal for the conversion of farmland to forestry in a deprived and remote area might be successful if jobs were created. By contrast, areas of 'preserved' countryside in southern England are often home to middle-class incomers who are much more likely to oppose proposed changes of land use.

# Rural population

**Q1** What are the age–sex characteristics of an expanding (repopulated) rural village in Europe and the USA?

**Q2** What types of worker might MEDC urban–rural migrants be?

**Q3** What are the age–sex characteristics of a declining (depopulated) rural village in Europe and the USA?

**Q4** How does ethnicity vary between urban and rural areas in the UK?

ANSWERS

# the age–sex, ethnic and occupational characteristics of people living in rural areas

A1 Above-average numbers of people in their thirties and forties; these 'incomers' also tend to bring young children

A2 Public sector workers (teachers, doctors); professionals who can telework from home using computers; tourism entrepreneurs; conservation workers

A3 An ageing population with a high dependency ratio, following the out-migration of economically productive people

A4 8% of Britain is non-white (4.6 million people). The figure rises to 60% in one London borough, but in rural areas is as low as 0.4%.

***examiner's* note** The distinction between expansion and decline is a useful starting point for analysis, as is that between 'rurban' (fringe) areas and remoter places. However, there are many rural 'types'; a series of different *ruralities* exists.

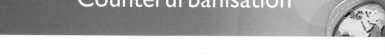

# Counterurbanisation

**Q1** What changes in rural areas of the UK and the USA have helped to attract new migrants since the late 1960s?

**Q2** In what ways might counterurbanisation be beneficial for existing rural communities?

**Q3** How might counterurban migration impact negatively upon existing rural communities?

**Q4** What are the economic costs of relocating to a rural area?

ANSWERS

## the relocation of people from urban to rural areas, beyond the suburbs

A1 Improvements to infrastructure (including electricity supply, road networks, telephone, radio, TV and mobile phone reception)

A2 Migrants support local services, pay taxes and help maintain school numbers; they may join clubs and societies

A3 Children of existing residents cannot always compete with affluent incomers in housing markets and may have to leave

A4 Removal costs; shops may charge higher prices; housing is expensive in desirable areas; some migrants face commuting costs

*examiner's* **note** The countryside is now highly differentiated. Some remote areas continue to lose population, while others are dominated by powerful landowners who block new housing development. Most counterurban migration has been into 'key settlements' that enjoy a range of basic services and easier access.

# Rural deprivation

**Q1** Why are employment opportunities very limited in some declining villages in rural Europe?

**Q2** Why are poor families in rural Europe often 'hidden from view'?

**Q3** Why might schools and shops still be closing in villages where populations are now rising as a result of counterurban migration?

**Q4** 1.2 billion people live in absolute poverty worldwide. What proportion of these live in rural areas?

**ANSWERS**

A1  Farming is now highly mechanised and tourism has not developed

A2  Average income statistics are boosted by middle-class incomers, concealing the persistence of deprivation among small sections of the original community that may lack saleable skills

A3  Migrants may drive to nearby towns for larger shops and schools, rather than supporting village services

A4  Three-quarters

***examiner's* note** Planners are increasingly concerned that lifestyles in some expanding villages in rural Europe are becoming increasingly polarised. Incomers buy older properties that possess attractive period features, such as thatched roofs, and occupy a central position. Older families, on lower incomes from farm work or seasonal tourism, often get displaced to areas of newly built rented housing on the outskirts.

# Working countryside

**Q1** Agriculture in Britain requires 73% of the land, but what contribution does it make to employment?

**Q2** Why have some rural areas of Europe that depend heavily upon tourism experienced falling visitor numbers in recent years?

**Q3** What is the financial disadvantage of working in rural tourism?

**Q4** What financial aid exists for new rural businesses in the UK?

ANSWERS

## a vision of rural areas that stresses their continuing productivity, not just their aesthetic qualities

A1 Only 2% of the working population is employed in agriculture

A2 They have been badly hit by a downturn in tourist numbers due to cheap overseas holidays, the credit crunch of 2008 and the continuing reluctance of American visitors to travel since 11 September 2001

A3 Seasonal unemployment (from October to March)

A4 Choose from: EU Structural Funds; UK government schemes (e.g. Rural Priority Areas); Regional Development Agencies; Scottish Local Enterprise Companies; charities and trusts

*examiner's* **note** Be aware of the environmental costs that a working countryside can bring. For instance, excessive use of nitrate fertilisers in East Anglia has sometimes resulted in widespread eutrophication in waters of the North Sea, drastically reducing lobster populations. More generally, uncontrolled use of pesticides such as DDT can bring harm to non-target species if they are transmitted through food webs.

# Intensive farming

**Q1** Which of these is not a form of intensive agriculture: market gardening, nomadic pastoralism or wet rice cultivation?

**Q2** Does intensive farming always give high yields per worker?

**Q3** The Indian Green Revolution increased yields through the adoption of HYVs such as IR-8. What does this mean?

**Q4** What environmental problems are associated with intensive forms of agriculture?

ANSWERS

A1  Nomadic pastoralism

A2  No. Wet rice cultivation gives high yields per unit area but requires large amounts of labour, thereby lowering the output per person.

A3  IR-8 is a high yielding variety (HYV) of rice, selectively bred to carry more grain per stalk

A4  Pesticides and nitrates in runoff; spread of disease in cattle; loss of biodiversity; loss of soil quality; concerns with GM (genetically modified) food

***examiner's* note** Attempts to boost food supply often involve a change from labour- to capital-intensive methods as machinery is introduced. Smallholders can be left landless as farm sizes are increased to improve efficiency. Changes that aim to reduce human suffering by improving farm outputs may therefore add to suffering by leaving large numbers of people unemployed and unable to buy food.

# Extensive farming

**Q1** Which of these is not always extensive agriculture: shifting cultivation, hill farming or commercial cereal farming?

**Q2** Why did forms of extensive agriculture such as cattle ranching develop rapidly during the twentieth century?

**Q3** Name a form of extensive farming that involves the periodic migration of the farmer.

**Q4** Which is more profitable: extensive or intensive farming? Why?

**ANSWERS**

## agriculture with low inputs of labour and/or capital per unit area

A1 Commercial cereal farming: there may be high inputs per unit area of fertiliser and possibly of pesticides

A2 Improvements in transport and refrigeration technologies allowed extensive use of large areas of land at a great distance from markets

A3 Shifting cultivation or transhumance

A4 Either. Yields per unit area are lower when extensive methods are used but the farms are a lot larger.

*examiner's* **note** Systems analysis can be usefully applied to agriculture. There are human inputs of labour and capital, as well as physical inputs of water, sunlight, nutrients and carbon dioxide. Outputs include crops, waste, and water and nutrient losses via runoff.

# Agricultural globalisation

**Q1** How has consumer demand helped drive the globalisation of food supply networks?

**Q2** Why has it become easier to meet these demands?

**Q3** Suggest three negative externalities associated with the globalisation of food supply networks.

**Q4** Why do poor countries not always benefit from the growth of these networks?

ANSWERS ▶▶

# the lengthening of food supply networks, driven by consumer demand in rich nations

A1 Demand for cheaper goods; demand for greater variety of goods; demand for fresh produce even when it is out of season

A2 Lower transport costs; fewer border controls (e.g. EU); refrigeration of perishables; growth of supermarket supply chains

A3 Spread of diseases such as foot-and-mouth; spread of pests such as the Colorado beetle; pollution increases due to transportation of goods ('food miles')

A4 Levies on imports protect farmers in rich nations. In the EU, the levy is the difference between the import price and a minimum price that has been guaranteed to European farmers.

***examiner's* note** Research the distance the products in your fridge have travelled. A shopping basket containing 20 fresh foods may have travelled 100 000 miles (with such items as sugarsnap peas from Guatemala or asparagus from Peru).

 **93** ANSWERS

# Agribusiness

**Q1** Name a non-commercial form of agriculture.

**Q2** Biotechnology research has led to increasing use of g............... m............... crops.

**Q3** Why might food consumption fall in an area where agricultural output is increasing?

**Q4** Concern over the environmental costs of industrialised farming has increased consumer demand for o............... produce.

ANSWERS

A1 Choose from: subsistence; crofting; slash and burn; nomadic pastoralism

A2 Genetically modified

A3 Production of non-food crops, such as tobacco and tea, has increased; food is exported; local people cannot afford to buy the food for sale locally

A4 Organic

***examiner's* note** The relationship between people, industrialised forms of agriculture and hunger is complex. For instance, per capita food production in Africa is now at 80% of the level it was in 1960. This reflects population growth but is also due to increased areas of land being turned over to the farming of non-food cash crops, such as coffee.

# Farm subsidy

**Q1** Since 1963, EU farmers have been subsidised by the CAP. What does CAP stand for?

**Q2** The CAP gives farmers a price guarantee. How does this work?

**Q3** The EU used to make payments to farmers who left their land fallow for 5 years. What was this policy known as?

**Q4** What is Countryside Stewardship?

ANSWERS

# financial support given to agriculture by government

A1 Common Agricultural Policy

A2 Minimum prices are set for arable crops. If the market price should fall below this, the EU will buy the crops from the farmer at the guaranteed minimum price.

A3 Set-aside

A4 A UK policy that provides grant aid for farmers who actively preserve environment and landscape

*examiner's* **note** Farm subsidies are increasingly controversial. They were originally introduced after the Second World War to boost productivity, but there are many negative externalities now associated with them. Over-production is often accompanied by environmental damage attributable to intensive methods. They may also contribute to poverty among LEDC farmers who cannot compete.

# Forestry and fishing

**Q1** Name two forest biomes.

**Q2** What is a 'post-industrial' forest used for?

**Q3** How many miles out to sea are fishing rights normally claimed by nations?

**Q4** Which technological developments have contributed to widespread growth of unsustainable fishing?

ANSWERS

# forms of primary activity, harvesting renewable natural resources

A1 Choose from: coniferous forest (boreal); tropical rainforest (selva); deciduous forest; mangroves

A2 Recreation and conservation, rather than timber production

A3 200 miles

A4 Larger factory trawlers equipped with refrigerators; bottom-trawling nets; sonar and radar technologies for locating shoals

***examiner's* note** Do not neglect these two important types of activity, particularly given that oceans cover two-thirds of the Earth's surface and forest accounts for about a quarter of the remainder. There are serious concerns about the long-term sustainability of both activities. Deforestation is responsible each year for the removal of an area of rainforest the size of the UK, and two-thirds of all north Atlantic commercial fish stocks are being used unsustainably.

# Tourism

**Q1** What economic risks does a predominantly tourist-based economy run?

**Q2** Which key factor is responsible for the huge growth in world tourism in recent decades?

**Q3** What additional factors have allowed the heightened demand for tourist activities to be met by tour operators?

**Q4** Why might a country not benefit economically from having large numbers of international visitors?

ANSWERS

## travel for recreation, health or religious reasons (tertiary sector)

A1  Tourist flows are easily disrupted by poor weather, war and political unrest, and competition from new destinations; individuals bear the risk of seasonal unemployment.

A2  Rising incomes in MEDCs and the growth of an affluent society

A3  Fast and cheap air flights; growth of marketing using media and the internet; improved education; fewer border controls (e.g. EU)

A4  Revenues from package tours return to the tourists' own countries

***examiner's* note** Tourism essays sometimes run the risk of becoming rather descriptive and of turning into travel diaries. Try to make links with other areas of human geography. Try to apply knowledge of globalisation and transnational corporations. Concepts such as service thresholds, tertiarisation and cumulative causation might also be relevant.

**(97) ANSWERS**

# Ecotourism

**Q1** Because the environment is not damaged, this is said to be a s............. form of tourism.

**Q2** If managed well, ecotourism brings benefits to local people, called i............. communities.

**Q3** Tourism that destroys the assets its growth is based on is unsustainable. Why may this be especially true of coastal resorts?

**Q4** Suggest two physical environments well suited to ecotourism.

ANSWERS

A1  Sustainable

A2  Indigenous

A3  Pollution of coastal waters from hotel sewage outlets is hard to
avoid (a particular problem in the Mediterranean)

A4  Choose from: tropical rainforest; mountain environments; Arctic
and Antarctic wilderness; volcanic environments (among others)

***examiner's* note** Sustainable ecotourism needs careful management to
ensure that the carrying capacity of local environments is not exceeded by
excessively high visitor numbers. Lasting damage may be done if local fragile
ecosystems lack resilience and cannot recover from damage (e.g. trampling).

# Butler's model of tourism

**Q1** The first three stages are called e_____, i_____ and d_____.

**Q2** Why are tourist numbers low at first, usually consisting only of members of an elite group?

**Q3** Why does stagnation eventually begin to occur?

**Q4** Increasing tourism for the world's remote regions is called growth of the p_____ p_____.

ANSWERS ▶▶

# a model suggesting a sequence of stages in the development of a tourist destination

A1 Exploration, involvement and development

A2 Infrastructure is not yet in place to transport or accommodate large numbers; costs are high, as economy of scale is lacking, restricting access to the affluent only

A3 Many people have already been there; newer and more fashionable destinations have been developed elsewhere

A4 Pleasure periphery

***examiner's* note** This is a useful model, but only when answering a question about the changes a tourist destination has experienced over time. Do not waste time reproducing the model in every essay about tourism, irrespective of the title. Little is to be gained, for instance, in making anything other than passing reference to it in an essay on the environmental consequences of world tourism.

# Rebranding

**Q1** Why do rural areas often need rebranding?

**Q2** Why do urban areas sometimes need rebranding too?

**Q3** With which sector of industry is rebranding associated?

**Q4** How can television help with the rebranding process?

ANSWERS

# redevelopment or marketing strategy aimed at changing people's perception of a place

A1  Countryside areas often suffer from a lack of jobs for young people owing to modern farming methods; rebranding brings new jobs in tourism

A2  Urban areas often suffer from a lack of jobs for young people owing to deindustrialisation; rebranding brings new opportunities

A3  Service or tertiary sector

A4  Areas that feature in popular shows can exploit this popularity, as fans of the show may wish to visit filming locations. Destinations may also be advertised on television

***examiner's* note** Rebranding can be a *contested* process. Not everyone living in a place will agree about the kind of image they want to project to the rest of the world. Glastonbury has been rebranded as a music festival town in recent years, but some local people object to this image. They would prefer to see the town exploit its religious and spiritual heritage.